LAWRENCE DALLAGLIO

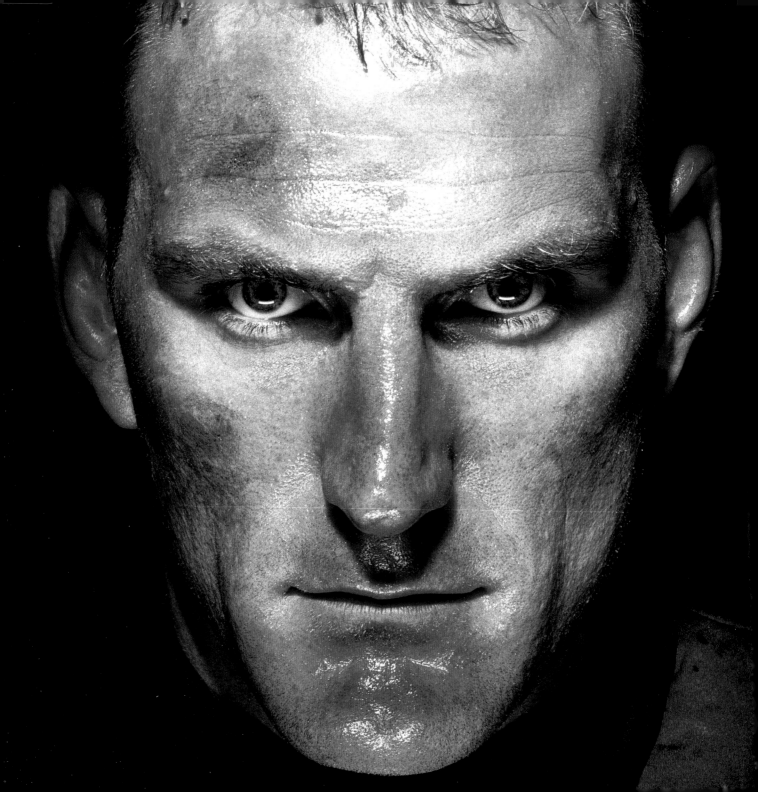

LAWRENCE DALLAGLIO

AN ILLUSTRATED HISTORY

CONTENTS

Created by Essential Works
168a Camden Street
London NW1 9PT

Pictures: Supplied by Getty Images
(except page 2 that appears courtesy
of celebritymediagroup.com)
Text: Chris Jones
Caption text: Iain Spragg
Editorial: Nell Chislett
Printed in Italy by STIGE

FOREWORD BY SIR STEVE REDGRAVE

When a well-known sportsman is given a testimonial you tend to ask yourself, what has he actually done to deserve such wonderful recognition, honour and tribute? Does he really deserve it? If you are like me, you examine the dedication and the commitment of that particular person to his club and country and you take a view.

In the case of Lawrence Bruno Nero Dallaglio, you immediately realise what a fantastic and devoted servant this man has been to London Wasps and what a superb warrior model he has been to his fellow professionals and to young players. Once you have seen Lawrence in a dramatic newspaper photo or on the TV, the image remains in your head, in your mind's eye. You think of chest-busting pride, of raw courage, of muscle-pumping determination. A glorious bull in a Number 8 shirt. A man with grit etched across his angular face and square jaw. And those steely eyes that silently tell his opponents: 'I'm a winner.' His 6ft 4ins of unconquerable power also motivates team-mates to raise their game – a quality you only find in great champions. Yet, off the pitch he is the gentle father of three children (Ella Francesca, Josie Mae and Louis Vincenzo) and partner to Alice. Domestically, he is the opposite of his on-field character.

His playing record is exceptional. In 1993, as a London Wasps flanker and aged only 20, he lifted the Sevens World Trophy for England, the first World Cup England had won since Wembley in 1966. He has captained Wasps, he has captained England. His career has steadily reached ever greater heights up to his personal pinnacle this year – playing for England in the Rugby World Cup in Australia. As a man, who, I know, still fancies himself as a white-suited John Travolta, he has graphically left his mark on the dance-floor of modern rugby.

Lol, I am proud to be both your friend and your fan.

Have a great year!

Yours

Sir Steve Redgrave CBE

FOREWORD BY JAMES R JULYAN

Lawrence Bruno Nero Dallaglio – a big name – a big man. Six feet four inches of power and muscle and a world class athlete. You don't, however, get the honour of a testimonial just for being big. Loyalty to your club is a major part, but achieving, giving your all and delivering when it matters is paramount. Lawrence Dallaglio joined Wasps in 1990 as a young man full of promise. Since then, he has delivered on that promise and shown us that he embodies qualities that are simply inspirational.

I am delighted that as a businessman from Gerrard and a rugby fan I have been asked to write a foreword for such an inspirational sportsman. Not only do the ties between rugby and Gerrard go back a long way, having had past presidents of RFUs and international players among our staff, but we, like Lawrence, aim to deliver. As a passionate follower and supporter of rugby, I have watched LD play for Wasps and for England over the years, and have always admired his ability and attitude on the pitch. Off the pitch, he is equally impressive. I first met Lawrence in the mid-nineties, when I invited him to speak at a conference I was hosting – and yes, he was brilliant at that too! He talked about leadership, pride and about making a difference in what you do. He touched on the need to triumph over adversity, to deal with setbacks and to come back even stronger.

In the business arena just as in the sports arena we too need qualities of pride, dedication, loyalty, passion, professionalism, courage and leadership. We look for success – we look for winners.

Who better than LD to be a role model, to demonstrate these qualities? Lawrence is a winner.

On the pitch he is a hard, determined, skillful and courageous player who evokes awe and respect from his opponents and team-mates alike.

Off the pitch he is a gentleman – friendly, easy-going and great company.

If individual and team success is knowing what you want and why you want it, what you must do to get it and, most importantly, DOING those things, then these pages will show you that LD does the things it takes.

Lawrence, you deserve this. My company and I are proud to be associated with you. Make it a great year and enjoy.

Regards

James R Julyan
Executive Director, Gerrard Ltd.

INTRODUCTION

Football-mad Lawrence Bruno Nero Dallaglio idolised George Best, Denis Law and Bobby Moore and that's why he was cradling a round ball when he arrived at Ampleforth School in North Yorkshire. Barely into his teens, Dallaglio's life was about to take a dramatic change as he suddenly realised that Ampleforth, famed for its Catholic education, worshipped another sporting religion: rugby union. 'I counted 27 sets of rugby posts,' explained Dallalgio. 'Not one pitch was marked out for football and so mine was quickly hidden from view.'

Born into an Anglo-Italian family, Dallaglio had been hugely influenced by his father, Vincenzo's, love of football, born out of a devotion to Juventus and kept alive by regular visits to Chelsea after he settled in this country and married Lawrence's mother, Eileen. Today, Chelsea still has a special place in Dallaglio's heart, thanks to those visits alongside his father, but thanks to Ampleforth, it is the oval ball that is the centre of his sporting world.

Eight years after making his England debut as a replacement against South Africa, Dallaglio has become a rugby icon, a man who has dealt with personal tragedy and the loss of the England captaincy, yet emerged stronger for the painful experience. Lesser men would have been broken by sadness and self-doubt, but this is no ordinary 31-year-old.

Fourteen years ago, the Dallaglio family lost Francesca, Lawrence's sister, when she died in the Marchioness disaster on the Thames at just nineteen years old. Dallaglio should have been on the boat, but illness meant that he stayed home on what was to become a night that changed his life forever. The immense sense of loss remains with him and his family, but through his rugby, Dallaglio has given himself and his parents something to focus on, a way of moving forward. He explains: 'My solution has always been to totally immerse myself in looking forward. I am still headstrong and feel that I am on a mission in general, not just rugby. At the time of my sister's death, rugby gave me a focus when it would have been easy to drift down a different path. Also, it provides a small bit of comfort to my parents.'

The rugby career that Dallaglio forged has brought World Cup Sevens glory, Grand Slam triumph with England, test series winning heroics with the Lions and league and cup success with London Wasps, the club that is woven into the fabric of his life. As a young man he hero-worshipped Zinzan Brooke, the All Black great, and now all over England, young back row forwards dream of being Dallaglio. He has overcome serious injury, the desperate disappointment of losing Grand Slams and even the notoriety of having to resign the England captaincy.

Throughout the good and bad times, Dallaglio has found comfort in the support of those closest to him: his parents Vincenzo and Eileen; Alice the mother of his three children, Ella, Josie Mae and Enzo; and friends who stayed true, whatever.

Now, the time has come to honour a remarkable athlete, a player who leads from the front for club and country, amassing thirteen tries in 58 England matches and is going into the World Cup of 2003.

While a testimonial year often signals the end of a career, in the case of the 1996 Rugby Football Union's Player of the Year, it's merely another chapter in a continuing story of a rugby legend.

Lawrence Dallaglio, we salute you and thank you for the pleasure that you've given us so far in your career.

Get the strength of Gerrard's investment team on your side.

If you're looking for a way to beef up the performance of your investment portfolio, why not put your money in the hands of Gerrard's team of specialists?

We are one of the UK's major players in wealth management, with all the resources necessary to help you make the most effective use of your money. And we offer:

- **A tailormade investment portfolio designed to achieve your financial goals**

- **A personal service, including your own individual investment manager**

- **A dedicated research team, and advanced market analysis technology, to identify investment opportunities around the globe**

- **A national network of local offices bringing City expertise to your doorstep**

For more information, and to arrange a meeting, please call our London office on:

0845 601 3218

Old Mutual Place, 2 Lambeth Hill, London EC4V 4GG

www.gerrard.com

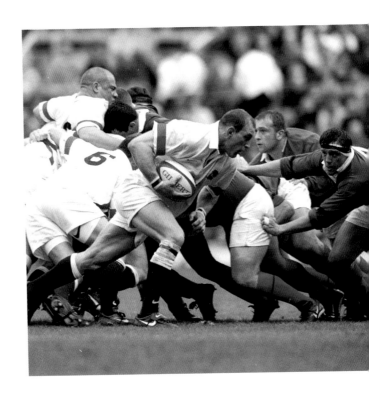

Gerrard
creating and managing wealth

1993
—
1997

Where were you when England won the World Cup? No, not the one in 1966 with 'people on the pitch who think it's all over'. We are talking about the one where a team of no-hopers were sent off to Murrayfield to make up the numbers and ended up winning the 1993 Rugby World Cup Sevens title. Lawrence Dallaglio knows where he was – right in the middle of the on-pitch celebrations by a ten–man squad that confounded the critics and their own Union to become masters of the world. Captain Andrew 'The Prince' Harriman had played once for England, but the other nine were new to the international stage. In the years that followed, all but two (Justyn Cassell and Dave Scully) would miss out on international honours but the others – Dallaglio, Chris Sheasby, Tim Rodber, Adedayo Adebayo, Damain Hopley, Nick Beal and Matt Dawson – would play test rugby for England.

However, the portents were not good for the squad as they lost to a side hastily put together by Dundee High School Old Boy's to offer the English match practise. The England management were incensed by the loss and wanted to know why that young lad called Dallaglio had been included. Harriman defended his team, informing the management that the whole squad had been out on the lash the night before to mark Hopley's birthday. The captain assured the coach and manager that things really would get better. They could hardly have got worse!

England's main weapon in the Sevens was Harriman's blistering pace. It would have been good enough to get him into the Olympics, but thankfully he chose rugby and, as Australia were to discover in the final, there is no answer to real pace. Harriman left Wallaby legend David Campese in his wake as England, with Dallaglio playing at prop, won the final and created rugby history. In typical Harriman style, he took the Melrose Cup from the Princess Royal, turned to her and had a quick chat. He said: 'I recalled that I had been in class with Prince Edward at Cambridge and asked for my best wishes to be passed on.'

Dallaglio followed this success with a Middlesex Sevens triumph for Wasps and having started the year as one of the successes on the England U21 tour to Australia the previous summer, he was suddenly making waves in the senior game. Not everything was going his way, though. Dallaglio was desperate to play for London against the touring All Blacks but the selectors went for Rory Jenkins. They wanted a more physical player at No7 they said. The thunderous look on Dallaglio's face after learning his fate made it very clear that here was a young player who would not settle for second-best. As the year drew to a close he said: 'My long-term ambition is to win a full cap for England and wearing the white shirt in the World Sevens has made me even more determined. But my first priority must be to break into the Wasps league team, so next season I'm going to switch from No8 to open-side, which is where people seem to think I will have the best chance of making my mark.'

Sevens rugby has always been close to Dallaglio's heart and that 1993 Cup victory helped raise his profile in England. In March this year, he was asked to join a President's XV at the Hong Kong Sevens, which included four team-mates from that Murrayfield triumph: Damian Hopley, Chris Sheasby, Nick Beal and Dave Scully.

Dallaglio forced his way into Wasps, Middlesex and London colours and then won a place on England's summer tour to South Africa, which meant the media wanted to know more about the 22-year-old. As he made a bigger impression on the game in England, it was inevitable that Dallaglio would attract media attention. All too often, of course, that means the rest of your life becomes very public. Inevitably, Dallaglio had to talk publicly about the loss of his sister Francesca in 1989. It was during this period that Dallaglio marked himself out as a young man with the ability to translate feelings into words with a confidence well beyond his years. Right from the start, he was happy to deal with the difficult issues.

Dallaglio had been asked to join his sister on the Marchioness but had been ill and declined. 'We discussed it the night before,' he said. 'My sister was going with her boyfriend and they said: "Well, are you coming?" I hadn't been feeling well. I left it to the last minute and decided not to go.' The Marchioness set sail without him on a voyage that was to claim 51 lives, among them Francesca, a nineteen-year-old ballerina. The fact that Dallaglio chose to live on a houseboat on the Thames raised even more questions for those trying to build up a picture of a back-row forward that England coach Dick Best had been insisting was quick enough to play in the backs. 'In a curious way I feel closer to her there,' said Dallaglio .'I go outside on the boat sometimes and think how things used to be.'

Dallaglio's rugby life was about to change forever as he headed to South Africa with England, after just ten first division matches for Wasps. It would be a tour that took him to the very limit in terms of anger management. He was part of the mid-week England side that was, effectively, beaten up by Eastern Province in Port Elizabeth. The match was ruined by the attitude of the home players and a referee totally out of his depth. Tim Rodber was sent off for retaliating and almost every England player had an injury by the final whistle. The casualty list included full-back Jonathan Callard (25 stitches in two deep cuts on his head), No8 Dean Ryan (broken bone in his right thumb which had to have four pins inserted) and prop Graham Rowntree (concussed after a heavy fall). Dallaglio and Bath prop John Mallett agreed to pose for photographs showing the red slashes on their backs caused by Eastern Province studs. On reflection, Dallaglio now wishes he hadn't let the photographs be taken because the locals considered it English whingeing. From that moment on, Dallaglio decided to take the hits and just keep getting up until the opposition wilted.

It was an attitude that would serve him well in the years to come.

You know the feeling. Everything seems to be going along very nicely and then it happens. Dallaglio was enjoying his season at Wasps, hoping to build on that tour to South Africa, when the rock on which he was basing a potentially brilliant career was suddenly shifting all over the place. The cause was a northern millionaire who wanted to turn Newcastle into a major sporting city, just like Barcelona. To do this, he bought in high-profile rugby players to help create a new team. Central to the birth of Newcastle RFC was Rob Andrew, the key figure at Wasps who had been runners-up in the Cup earlier in the year. When he jumped ship, the England outside-half took fellow internationals Dean Ryan and Steve Bates with him. Suddenly, Wasps needed a new captain and the finger of fate pointed at Dallaglio. He was 23 years old.

The emergence of Lawrence has been great for the club and England,' said Rob 'Hector' Smith, the Wasps coach. 'He has a lovely manner about him and a tremendous will to win.' It was an inspired choice and gave Dallaglio the added profile that wasn't going to harm his chances when England coach Jack Rowell was looking around to rebuild his team after the 1995 Rugby World Cup (having opted not to include Dallaglio in that squad). Four-try Jonah Lomu had destroyed England in the Cup semi-finals in Cape Town and when the autumn internationals came around, Rowell gave the new Wasps captain his debut as a replacement against South Africa at Twickenham.

He took over from Tim Rodber and created a try for Phil de Glanville, a player who would be vying for the England captaincy with Dallaglio in the years to come. 'I didn't want the game to end, although the others may have felt differently. It was really good fun,' said the new cap afterwards. It was considerably more fun than the task Dallaglio had to face back at the team hotel. He received that coveted first cap in a rather subdued England dressing room after the Springboks defeat and then it was back to the hotel for the ritual all debutants have to endure.

'You are supposed to take a drink from every team-mate but I only got half way around the guys,' admitted Dallaglio. 'A pathetic effort really!' With professional rugby only just starting to take hold, it was back down to earth with a bump 48 hours later for Dallaglio, still an amateur player. He returned to Kingston University and the final year of an Urban Estate management course.

It can't have been all that bad though, because it was at Kingston that Dallaglio met Alice Corbett, the woman who was to share his many highs and lows during an extraordinary rugby career and provide him with three children. However, at this point, he was still playing the role of a Twickenham-based student, living on his houseboat called Bardot, moored near the town centre. England coach Rowell made sure Dallaglio's profile would rise in 1996, however, by stating: 'I believe that Lawrence is a young man who in a year, subject to gaining more test experience, can become a lead singer for England.'

November was a remarkable period in Dallaglio's rugby life, with a second cap against Samoa, and he picked up the Evening Standard Player of the Month award – a bronze statuette and a magnum of Laurent-Perrier pink champagne.

This year, Dallaglio, already being described as 'England's captain-in-waiting' signed a new contract with Wasps following the arrival of Chris Wright, head of Chrysalis, as the club's new owner. This was hardly surprising as Dallaglio had been voted England's Player of the Year and Wright was bullish about the future for a club that he was going to merge into Loftus Road plc with Queens Park Rangers football club. Wright said: 'We hope to be doing good business at Loftus Road by playing the big Wasps games there, so generating the revenue to pay the top players. It is crucial that Dallaglio remains a cornerstone of the new Wasps.' Little did Wright realise that in the years to come it would be the rugby club, led by Dallaglio, that was going to give him happy days, while QPR supplied the heartache and abuse from disgruntled fans. Dallaglio had other offers from top English clubs but proved, yet again, that Wasps was in his heart.

Jack Rowell eventually named Bath's Phil de Glanville as the new England captain and Dallaglio said: 'Of course I hoped for one small second it might be me. Others in the game had intimated they thought it would be. I didn't feel I lacked anything. I think the feeling was that at 24, I needed a bit more time.' Ex- England coach Dick Best, who had seen the potential in Dallaglio when he was still a second team player at Wasps, set out the challenge for both the player and England before the autumn international with Italy. 'After a full international season last year, Dallaglio must now make the No7 jersey his own and become the key to unlocking the fifteen-man game England aspire to,' he said. Working out which of the back row numbers best suited the Wasps star would be a constant problem for various England coaches because he was equipped to play at No8, open-side flanker and blind-side. Dallaglio rose to Best's challenge brilliantly in the end of year jamboree playing for England against the New Barbarians – who were effectively the All Blacks in disguise. He scored two tries in an England defeat witnessed by a full house at Twickenham, filled with supporters who also recognised the emergence of a truly great back-row forward who cared little for reputations or the emblem on their jerseys.

This was a defining twelve months for Dallaglio on and off the pitch. In March Alice gave birth to Ella Francesca, their first daughter, and by July she would be on the other side of the world as her proud father played in one of the most ludicrously organised England matches in history.

Besides becoming a father, 1997 was all about gaining selection for the Lions tour to South Africa under coach Ian McGeechan. Having missed out on the 1995 World Cup in that country, this was Dallaglio's chance to prove to one of the greatest rugby nations on earth that he was a world-class forward. It would be a long hard process to win selection and even tougher to make the test side, though. It all started well on a personal note for Dallaglio, with a signature try in a home 23-20 defeat by France. The image of Dallaglio striding through the French defence with the kind of pace not normally associated with a big forward immediately caused a stir amongst the ranks of England fans.

The championship would end in disappointment for Dallaglio who failed to face Wales in what was the final match at the old Arms Park Stadium. As a student of the game, he was gutted at missing this moment of rugby history, but he was in no fit state to be anywhere else but his Cardiff hotel room, feeling very ill. 'I was feeling absolutely awful,' he explained. 'At the time, it was hugely disappointing because it would have been very special – a true rugby experience.' It was to be a fleeting feeling of rugby gloom as he led Wasps to the Courage League title with a 26-15 win at Northampton and was selected for that Lions tour to South Africa.

The test series was won 2-1 with Dallaglio joining fellow England stars Richard Hill and Tim Rodber in a brilliant back row, but before he could really enjoy the moment, it was onto another plane and off to Australia for that ridiculous match. To play the test, the Rugby Football Union flew nine players 22 hours from London to link up with sixteen others who had travelled sixteen hours from South Africa (via Harare and Perth) after helping the Lions win the series. No surprisingly, England lost 25-6 and it marked the end of Phil de Glanville's reign as captain. Also exiting stage left was Jack Rowell as coach, allowing the arrival of Clive Woodward, the man who would help Dallaglio through the toughest time in his life – but that was still to come.

In the aftermath of the Sydney debacle, I wrote in the Evening Standard: 'England have no option but to appoint Lawrence Dallaglio as captain and base their 1999 World Cup campaign around the best back-row in the Northern Hemisphere.' And they did. However, he was handed the hospital pass of all time with his first four test matches as captain against South Africa, Australia and New Zealand (twice). Draws with Australia and New Zealand, plus defeats by the All Blacks and South Africa proved, if nothing else, that he could lead by example. For Dallaglio, those results were not good enough though, and he said: 'I hate losing and I want to be captaining a winning England team. Unlike in 1993, when we thought a one-off win against New Zealand proved everything was right in our game, we won't be papering over the cracks this time. We have to make a quantum leap to get into the first division of international rugby and at the moment we are in the second division. My target is to help England get to the top of the first.' They

LAWRENCE DALLAGLIO

previous pages:
left Making strides. Dallaglio cuts through the Northampton defence in the final of the 1993 Middlesex Sevens at Twickenham.

right Walloping the Wallabies. Dallaglio in action during England's surprise 1993 World Cup Sevens final win over the Aussies at Murrayfield.

these pages:
left Action man. At the Dubai Sevens, Dallaglio learns that the grass isn't always greener. More like a sandy brown.

right Dallaglio is hauled back by two Western Samoa tacklers during the Hong Kong Sevens in 1994.

1993–1997

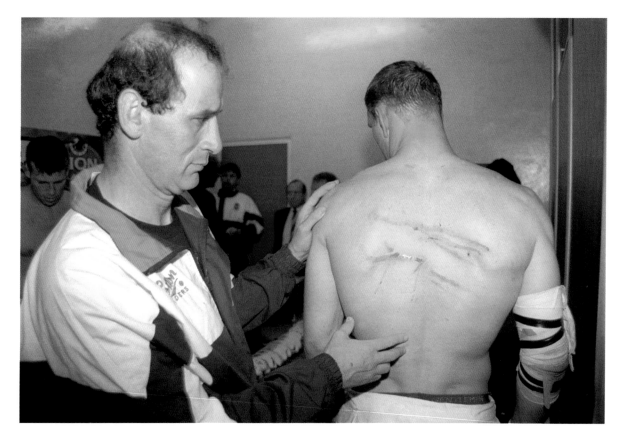

above No pain, no gain. England doctor Terry Crystal inspects the damage.

right Dallaglio in full flight for Wasps against Bath in the Courage League.

left Soon to be a familiar sight, a young Dallaglio in an England shirt in April 1994. Nice hair.

right Good leap, shame about the ball. Dallaglio 'in training' with the rest of the England squad in 1995 in Lanzarote.

28   Competing for the ball in the 1995 Pilkington Cup
semi-final against Leicester. Wasps beat the
Tigers 25-22.

LAWRENCE DALLAGLIO

left 'I'm flying!' The 1996 Five Nations clash with Wales.

above Proving just how seriously modern players take rehydration after England beat Ireland at Twickenham.

Your place or mine? Dallaglio proudly shows off his London houseboat in 1996.

Before turning professional, Dallaglio gave serious consideration to a career in modelling. Thankfully, he made the right choice.

left Mean and moody. And lovely eyes!

above Dallaglio with his 1996 RFU Player
of the Year Award.

above Flag day. Dallaglio leads out Wasps for a Courage League Division One clash with Saracens at Loftus Road.

right Dallaglio shrugs off the tackle of a very small Frenchman on his way to the try line in the 1997 Five Nations clash at Twickenham. The French, however, still went on to win 23-20.

1993-1997

left Just hanging around. In league action against Northampton in 1997.

right Happy, smiling people. Dallaglio celebrates with coach Nigel Melville after Wasps clinch the 1997 Courage League Division One Championship.

LAWRENCE DALLAGLIO

far left Lion tamers. Dallaglio bursts through during the Lions 35-30 defeat to Northern Transvaal in Pretoria on the 1997 tour to South Africa.

left In the same game, Dallaglio rises highest but it was not enough to save the Lions' blushes.

above Missing Blues Brother located.

right Dallaglio the scrum-half as the Lions narrowly beat the Springboks 18-15 in the second Test at Kings Park, Durban, to wrap up a famous series win.

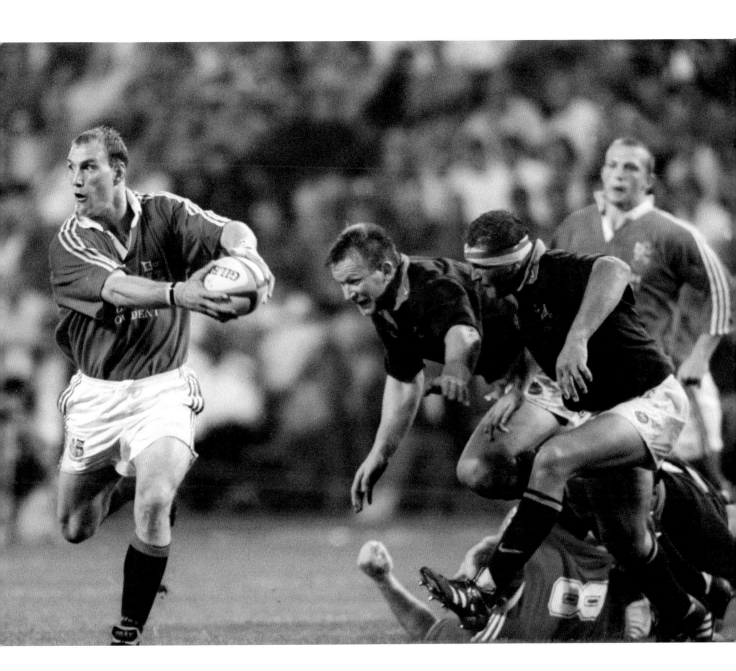

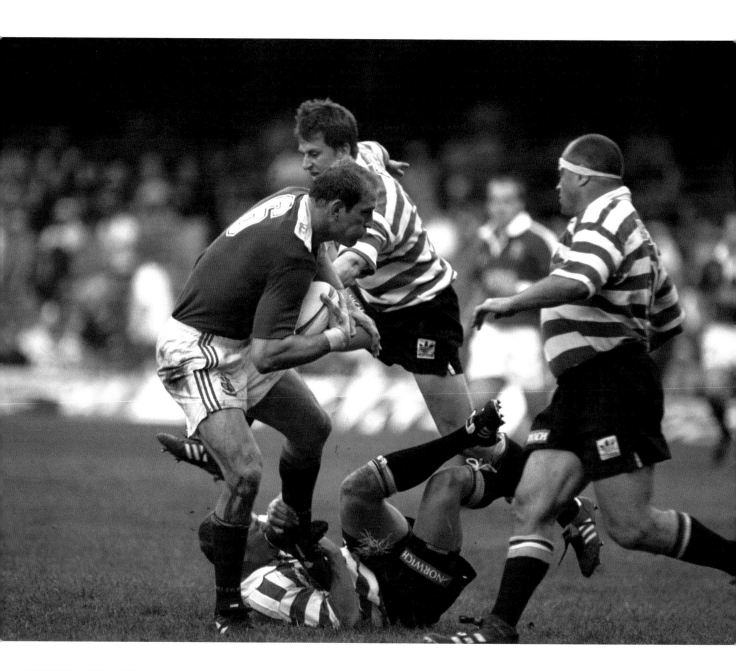

LAWRENCE DALLAGLIO

left Don't you just hate it when you get something stuck to your foot? Dallaglio takes on Western Province at Newlands.

right Beach bums. Dallaglio takes time out with fellow Lions Richard Hill and Tim Rodber on Blouberg Strand.

left Good job she looks like her mother! With Alice and baby Ella in 1997.

right A proud moment as Dallaglio leads England out for the first time as captain for the Cook Cup clash with Australia at Twickenham in November 1997. The match ended in a 15-15 draw.

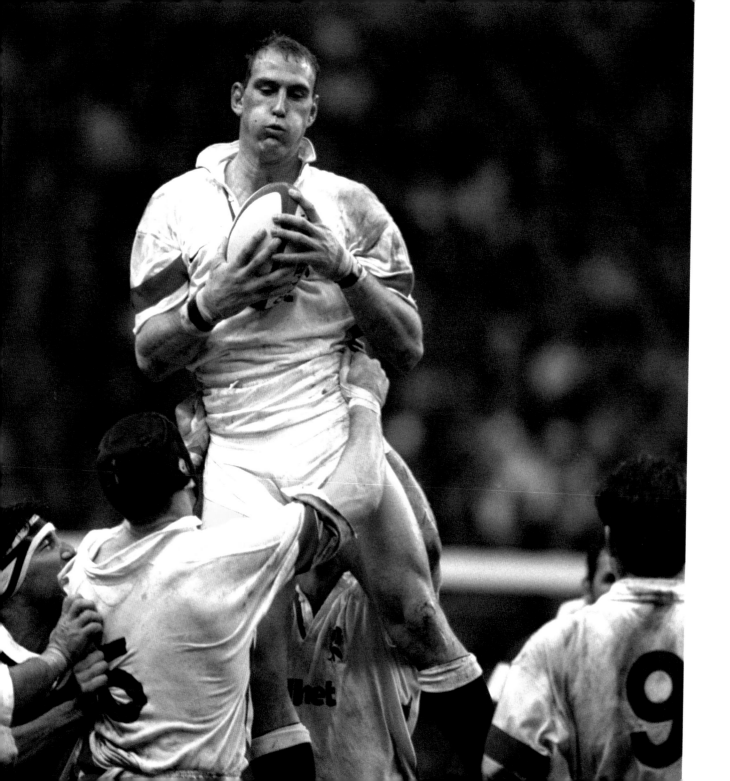

these pages:
left In action against the Wallabies.

right Rousing the troops during England's 25-8 reverse against the All Blacks in November 1997 at Old Trafford.

following pages:
left Catch me if you can. Dallaglio leaves New Zealand in his wake at Old Trafford.

right Watch where you're putting your hands! Dallaglio has a lucky escape during England's defeat to the All Blacks.

LAWRENCE DALLAGLIO

1993-1997

photo © Jenny Goodall

ASSOCIATED NEWSPAPERS

WISH LAWRENCE A SUCCESSFUL BENEFIT YEAR

Daily Mail

The Mail ON SUNDAY

Evening Standard

FREE METRO

Baker Tilly - proud supporters of
The Lawrence Dallaglio Benefit Year

Even the best business needs a good sense of direction.

At Baker Tilly we help growing businesses focus on what to do to succeed.

Our particular expertise is in helping owner managed, entrepreneurial and growing businesses to achieve their ambitions.

For further information please contact:
Glyn Francies, Partner
Telephone: 01923 816400
Email: Watford@bakertilly.co.uk

www.bakertilly.co.uk

BAKER TILLY
INTERNATIONAL

BAKER TILLY

o2.co.uk

15 thorns in one side

ENGLAND RUGBY

O2

Tetley's are proud to support Lawrence Dallaglio in his Testimonial Season

1998
–
2002

1998

As starts go, it was awful. England lost 24-17 in France on the opening day of the championship and coach Clive Woodward was left still searching for a first win in charge of the national side. Captain Dallaglio was determined to give him one to remember and at the end of the clash with Wales at Twickenham, the scoreboard read England 60 Wales 26. The record books had been rewritten and Woodward wore the smile of a much-relieved man. After helping his team score eight tries against the hapless Welsh, Dallaglio said: 'I believe we have class players, great players, and we will become a great side.' No one was arguing that evening as the players headed off to mark Jeremy Guscott's 50th cap, although Phil Vickery's celebrations after his debut were muted as the Gloucester prop was cited for punching.

The championship match with Ireland featured a rare incident in Dallaglio's career when he refused to shake an opponent's hand. Irish flanker David Corkery had been spouting forth before the game about 'arrogant English' and Dallaglio turned his back when a hand was proffered at the end of the match that brought England a fourth consecutive Triple Crown. For Dallaglio, things were just hotting up, though, because of a club-or-country row surrounding the summer tour to Australia, South Africa and New Zealand.

Lions team manager Fran Cotton leapt to Dallaglio's defence over the taunts of 'Judas' aimed at the Wasps captain when he faced Saracens. 'To talk about one of our great players like that is totally insulting,' he said. 'Every one of us should be looking up to our England captain instead of insulting him. I'm very sad that these things have been said.' It was, however, a sign of the times as the RFU and the top clubs constantly battled for supremacy and the players got caught in the middle.

Dallaglio and a host of top players did not tour and even coach Woodward had harsh words for his captain after having to pick 17 uncapped players in the tour squad. 'As captain, Lawrence has been fantastic,' he said, adding, 'but I'm not going to put myself in a corner and say he will be straight back into the side. He was a shadow of himself in the Cup Final (Wasps lost 48-18 to Saracens) and I think Wasps made a mistake playing him. They picked a guy who was not fit and I think that's wrong. He needs a six-month rest.'

It was a hard time for Dallaglio, who hated letting his team leave these shores without him and he admitted: 'It hurts me not to be able to play, but the Southern Hemisphere is no place for passengers. I have a lot of confidence in my ability and, after a complete break, I will make sure I do myself justice next season.' He would miss the World Cup qualifiers in Huddersfield against Holland and Italy later in the year because of knee trouble, but returned to test action in November. South Africa were beaten 13-7 in an epic contest at Twickenham and only a controversial penalty robbed England of victory over Australia 12-11. 'We did more than enough to win – we should have won,' lamented the captain.

Some years just stick in the memory. This is the one that will always carry vastly differing emotions for Dallaglio. Josie Mae, his second daughter, arrived in May, while a Grand Slam opportunity lost in the dying moments against Wales at Wembley combined with attacks from Sunday newspapers would require him to resign from the job of England captain. It had all started so well though, with the England team sweeping towards the deserved first Grand Slam since Will Carling's men had achieved that goal in 1995. That was also a World Cup year and with Wales staging the tournament and the final in Cardiff, it looked as if England were going to be real contenders. What better way to signal your Cup challenge than by winning the Slam?

However, as rugby history now tells, it was the Welsh who somehow managed to emerge victorious 32-31, playing away from home because their Millennium Stadium was still being finished for the World Cup. Dallaglio's decision not to ask Jonny Wilkinson to kick for goal and, instead, go for touch, was a major turning point, with Welsh coach Graham Henry saying: 'If they had kicked that penalty it would have given them a buffer of nine points. They kicked for touch because they thought they would drive us over from the lineout.'

In the aftermath of the Slam defeat, Dallaglio found himself the victim of a Sunday newspaper sting on 23 May in which he said things he shouldn't have, and brought enough bad publicity upon himself, his family and the sport to have broken a lesser man. He resigned the captaincy the next day. When Dallaglio eventually appeared before an RFU inquiry, he pleaded guilty to bringing the game into disrepute and was fined £15,000. Throughout this period, Woodward stood by his side, even while offering observations such as: 'He's been a pratt.' However, the verdict was delivered by a man who never lost faith in Dallaglio and the pair would soon be back working together at test level.

It had been Woodward who opened his front door to give Dallaglio and his young family refuge when the scandal first broke. Woodward included Dallaglio in the World Cup preparations and Dallaglio said: 'Clive has been a rock, unlike many other people who I thought might have supported me. I'm eternally grateful to him for his support. The best way I can repay that is to perform as well as I possibly can.' For those close to Dallaglio, the end of this tough period was a blessed relief. Now, attention finally turned to a World Cup that Dallaglio desperately wanted to play well in.

When he pulled on the England jersey again against USA it coincided with the tenth anniversary of his sister Francesca's death in the Marchioness riverboat tragedy. 'I am fortunate to have a very strong family who have endured a great deal that was far worse than this,' he said. 'We all have a strong faith and I was deeply touched and surprised by the amount of support I received from the public.' The rehabilitation at test level was a major success but the challenge for the Cup ended in a hail of drop goals by Jannie de Beer that gave South Africa victory in Paris in the quarter-finals. Now, it was Dallaglio backing Woodward in his time of need with ex-captain Will Carling calling for the coach to go. 'Will is entitled to his opinion but in this case he is a long way off the mark. Clive has the total respect of all the players in the England squad. It's as simple as that.'

2000

The year started spectacularly at international level, with a win over Ireland and then one of England's bravest rugby rearguard actions that secured a hard fought triumph over France in Paris with Dallaglio at the heart of the defence. His reward was a knee injury that had cleared up in time for him to cross the try-line in an easy win over the Welsh at Twickenham and then came a first visit in the Six Nations Championship to Italy, birthplace of his father.

Before Dallaglio could head to Rome though, his father had to visit the Italian consulate to pick up a special exemption form to ensure his son was not called up for national service by the Italian authorities. Dallaglio missed national service by a couple of months, having turned 27 in August last year. Vincenzo had devised a plan in case the exemption was turned down and said: 'I would have said he cannot join up until after the final whistle of the game with Italy!' For Dallaglio, missing out on a spell in the army was a great relief and he admitted as much. 'The relevant form will now be permanently on the record and I wasn't looking forward to one of those short military haircuts because it's already short enough, thank you,' he half-joked. His mother Eileen was sitting alongside Dad in the stand in Rome wearing her red hat and carrying a Union Jack.

With Italy easily beaten it was off to Murrayfield for a second successive Grand Slam attempt, only for the heavens to open and England mess it up. Dallaglio scored an early try but the team made tactical errors and then forgot to accept the Six Nations trophy from the Princess Royal to make a dreadful day even worse. At least Wasps retained the Cup, beating Northampton 31-23 and Dallaglio signed a new contract even though Wasps had seen their old ground at Sudbury sold. They became gypsies, moving from one training ground to another until settling in Acton.

England headed to South Africa and were robbed of victory in the first test in Pretoria but came back to record a famous 27-22 win over the Springboks in Bloemfontein thanks to Jonny Wilkinson's boot. However, England's players were forced to go on strike in November before facing Argentina to get an increased match fee and Dallaglio, Matt Dawson and captain Martin Johnson emerged as the players' spokesmen. They beat the Pumas, South Africa and Australia at Twickenham and then Dallaglio captained an international team for the first time since resigning from the England job, when he led the Barbarians against South Africa in Cardiff in December. It was a great way to end a year of huge rugby highs and that low of having to go on strike for a better deal from the Rugby Football Union.

There were lighter moments this year though, including his inclusion in a list of the World's Most Sexy Men – which had Robbie Williams at No1. Fellow sexy sports stars included Andre Agassi, Lennox Lewis and Greg Rusedski.

2001

England appeared to be heading for Grand Slam glory after two bitter Slam disappointments. France, Wales, Scotland and Italy were all taken care of, only for the Foot and Mouth outbreak to force the game with Ireland to be postponed until October – after the Lions tour to Australia. It would prove to be a desperately unfortunate delay. For Dallaglio, this year became a frustrating injury nightmare in May. He was charging forward trying to get Wasps into the play-off finals of the Zurich Premiership against Bath when he sustained a knee injury.

It had already been a difficult season for Wasps, who finished runners-up in the league. Loftus Road plc hit financial troubles, thanks to the huge losses incurred by QPR. Wasps were dragged into the mire – although owner Chris Wright would eventually buy the rugby club and ensure its future, choosing Wasps over his former love QPR. This was hardly surprising, given the happy days at Twickenham that Wasps had given Wright while all he had got for the millions spent on QPR was even greater abuse from the fans.

Dallaglio kept his head down during the Loftus Road problems because he had a far greater personal worry following that knee ligament injury. It happened just a month before the Lions left for their tour of Australia and Dallaglio had to convince the Lions' insurance company that he was fit to get onto the plane for Perth.

There were moments of light relief for the Lions who had brought in a motivational company that insisted on turning the squad into a samba band – with coach Graham Henry on tambourine, captain Martin Johnson on maracas and Dallaglio having to come to terms with the hugely demanding bells. However, it wasn't until the insurance company gave the green light that Dallaglio could really feel part of the squad, and he said: 'The insurance company's medical team came to the hotel and gave me, effectively, an MOT. If I had not passed then I could not have toured because playing without insurance would not have been fair to Wasps or myself.' As it turned out, the knee wasn't completely right and although Dallaglio did play on tour, he was forced to return home early and enter hospital for surgery that would keep him out of rugby for seven months.

The long and difficult road back from surgery was made easier by the help and understanding of Dave 'Otis' Reddin, the England team's fitness expert who has done so much great work behind the scenes to help the national squad. Dallaglio worked one-to-one with Reddin at Twickenham, away from the media and fans, who all wanted to know when the big man would be back.

A very little man arrived to also make life more enjoyable for Dallaglio, in the form of Louis Vincenzo, born on 13 October, and he was an immediate hit with his two sisters. His arrival helped take Dallaglio's mind off events in Dublin where England were beaten 20-14 by the Irish and another Slam chance had been lost, compounding the view that England just couldn't win the big ones away from home. Key players, including Johnson and Matt Dawson, were also injured and couldn't play against the Irish, but mitigating circumstances weren't taken into consideration when the flack started flying.

2002

A year during which injury would once again rear its head before Dallaglio finally got onto the Twickenham pitch for his 50th cap against Australia, started with the Wasps captain getting dressed up as a crusading knight, complete with chain mail armour and the cross of St George. No, it wasn't Dallaglio's attempt to ward off any more injury problems – he was, in fact, a guest at Mike Catt's wedding which required all those invited to wear something rather outlandish.

Jeremy Guscott wore a smart black full-length coat and paisley cravat, while Catt's Bath colleague Iain Balshaw and two friends were dressed as the three musketeers, with swashbuckling swords and masks. When the party was over, the inevitable question was asked of our man: 'Lawrence, when are you going to play?' Dallaglio made the mistake of setting dates for his comeback and the media inked them into the diary, only for the knee.

A return at test level was delayed until the away game with Italy at the end of the championship, when something very unusual happened. Dallaglio was one of four England captains on the replacements bench! They were Martin Johnson, Jason Leonard, Matt Dawson and Dallaglio, who between them held 326 caps compared to the 372 amassed by the entire team that started the game. They all came onto the pitch at the same time and Dallaglio was back in the big time nearly a year after the initial injury against Bath.

He was rewarded by being handed the England captaincy for the first time since his resignation back in 1999, in the match with the Barbarians and the summer tour to Argentina – only for hand surgery on a damaged ligament to force him to withdraw. He didn't give up, of course. 'My next chance of an England cap is against New Zealand on 9 November at Twickenham and it's a great target to have.' And no-one was going to forget about him. Before the arrival of the All Blacks, Dallaglio linked up with fellow stars Kenny Logan and Keith Wood to launch an Eden Park shop in Richmond which saw their faces on adverts on the back of scores of London buses.

Dallaglio made it into the team for the 31-28 win over the All Blacks and the scene was set for his 50th appearance against Australia. Tradition means you lead the team out when reaching the milestone – but only if you actually start the match. For Dallaglio, the team announcement was a bitter disappointment with the Wasps captain relegated to the bench. He did win that 50th cap as a replacement. 'Talk about mixed emotions,' said Dallaglio. 'This was a fantastic win (32-31) against Australia, although the flip side of the coin is that when I came on just after half-time, I didn't make quite the impact I intended on my 50th cap. As a spectator behind me said when I returned to the bench after Richard Hill's blood-bin injury: "Dallaglio, we were winning before you went on."' He was on as a replacement as early as the 14th minute for the famous 53-3 victory over South Africa which gave England the scalps of every major nation a year before the World Cup, although the Springboks almost took home some scalps of their own. Corne Kirge, their captain, was shown in one sequence on Sky television delivering a forearm smash to the head of Dawson, following this with a knee into Dallaglio's back and then running at full pace to stamp on Phil Vickery. South Africa's full-back Werner Greef also kneed Dallaglio in the back.

Who said test rugby was easy? At least Dallaglio scored one of England's seven tries.

above August 1998. Suggestions that the England pack are too small are laughed off by the players.

right October 1998. Dallaglio with coach Clive Woodward at a press conference to announce his reappointment as England skipper.

far right 'And if I stand here, they'll never be able to kick for goal...'

left High rise. Dallaglio towers above everyone during Wasps' Premiership clash with Gloucester in October 1998.

right In action against the Australians in the 1998 Cook Cup at Twickenham. The Wallabies edged England 12-11.

below After beating the Springboks 13–7 at Twickenham, Dallaglio accepts Clive Woodward's Daz doorstep challenge.

right Poetry in motion. Dallaglio gives South Africa the runaround during England's win at Twickenham in December 1998.

'Get that stupid tracksuit off!' Dallaglio gives Victor Ubugo an earful before England's 32-31 defeat to Wales at Wembley in the 1999 Five Nations.

above Facing the media.

right Flanked by his legal team, Dallaglio answers his critics.

1998-2002

LAWRENCE DALLAGLIO

left That's my boy. Dallaglio congratulates Matt Perry as Italy are put to the sword at Twickenham in the 1999 World Cup.

right 'Just one pint for me, cheers…'

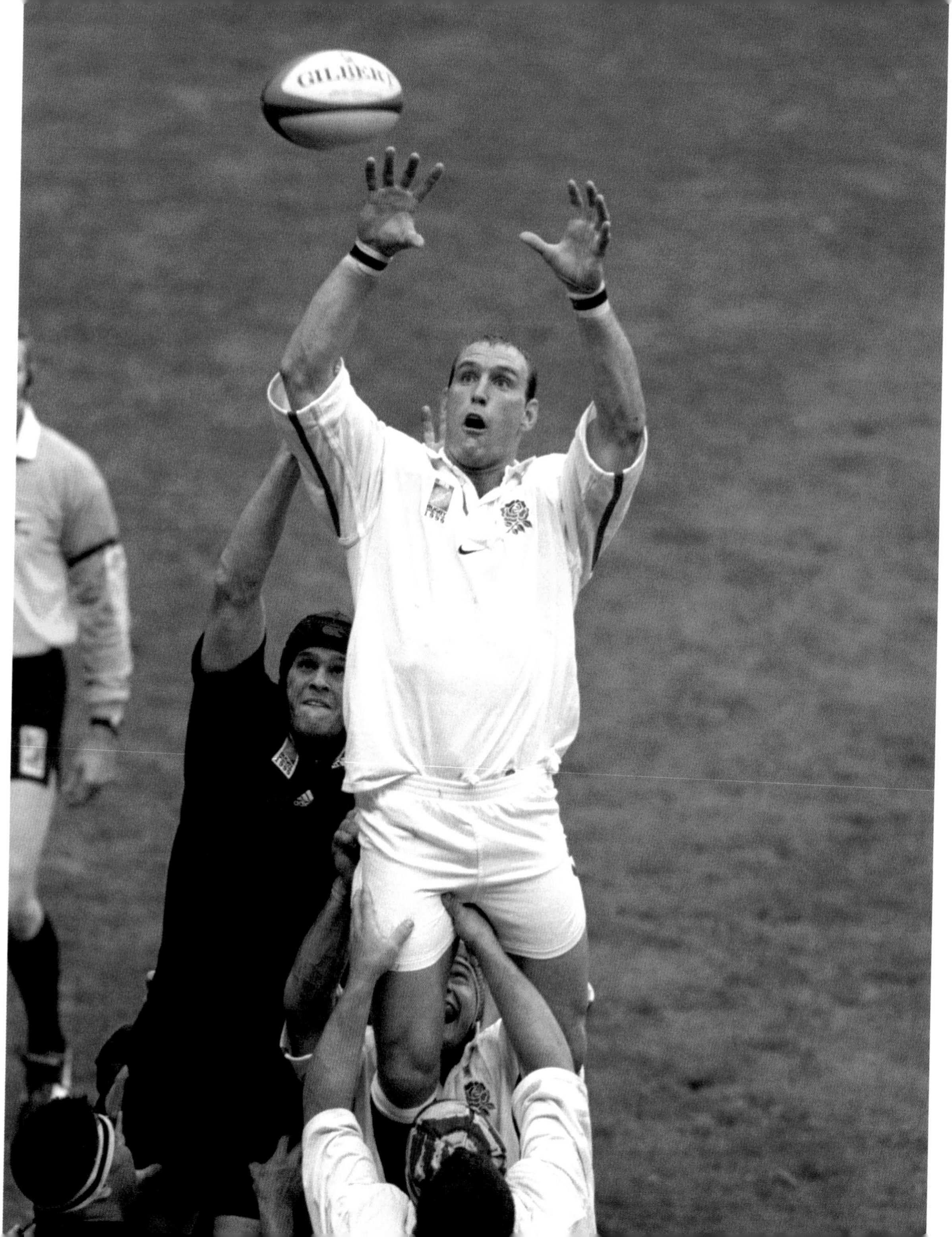
GILBERT

these pages:

left All Black and blue. In action at Twickenham against New Zealand in the World Cup. The All Blacks won 30-16.

above Stoop to conquer? Dallaglio feels the pressure as New Zealand prove too strong for England.

following pages:

left Bursting through against Fiji in the World Cup quarter-final play-off. England booked their place in the last eight with a 45-24 victory.

right Shattered dreams. Dallaglio and England crash out of the World Cup after losing 44-21 to South Africa in the quarter-final in Paris.

LAWRENCE DALLAGLIO

previous pages:
left The 2000 Six Nations. Dallaglio hears his lottery numbers have come up!

right Dallaglio takes Scotland's Andy Nicol for a ride.

these pages:
left Brothers in arms. Dallaglio, Danny Grewcock and Martin Johnson before England's 27-22 win over South Africa in Free State Stadium, Bloemfontein, in June 2000.

left Dallaglio gives it the thumbs up as Wasps tackle Gloucester in September 2000.

right Dallaglio suddenly realises how frightening the ball really is.

LAWRENCE DALLAGLIO

left Hunted down. Dallaglio can't escape the clutches of England team-mate and Leicester Tiger prop Graham Rowntree.

right 'Do you use conditioner?' Head-to-head with Gloucester's Phil Vickery at the launch of the 2001 Zurich Premiership.

left Final preparations for the 2001 Lions tour to Australia.

above Oarsome! Dallaglio tries his hand at dragon boat racing in the exotic Surrey countryside.

LAWRENCE DALLAGLIO

far left Team building Lions-style in May 2001 with Austin Healey and Phil Vickery.

left 'I could have played for Chelsea, you know.' Dallaglio shows Claudio Ranieri what he's been missing.

Lawrence prepares to test just how oval the Manly Oval in
Sydney really is on the Lions tour Down Under.

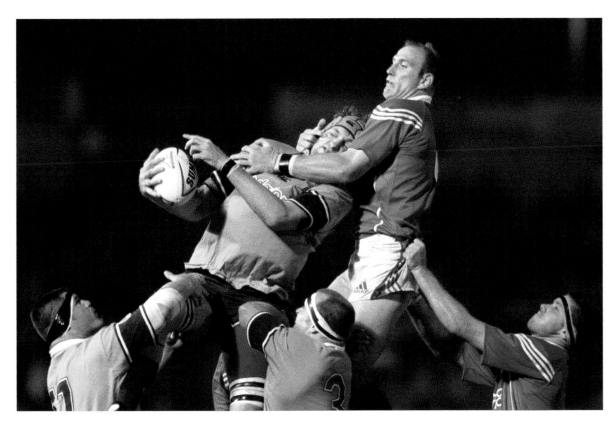

'I think you'll find that's my ball.' The Lions tackle
Australia 'A' in Gosford.

left Staring defeat in the face. Dallaglio watches from the bench as the Lions go down 28-25 to Australia 'A'.

right Dallaglio provides the fireworks for the Lions in Australia.

left Hands up if you want the ball! Dallaglio applies the pressure during the Lions clash with New South Wales in Sydney.

top right Assessing the damage. Dallaglio, seconds after picking up the knee injury which prematurely ended his Lions tour.

bottom right Heading home. Dallaglio reflects on what might have been before flying back to England.

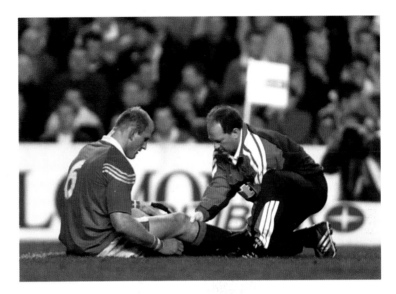

above 'But Jonny Wilkinson makes it look so easy!' Playing rugby Subbuteo at the Museum of Rugby, Twickenham, against England women's skipper Paula George.

right Laying down the law. Dallaglio tells it like it is as Wasps tackle Glasgow in the 1997 Heineken Cup.

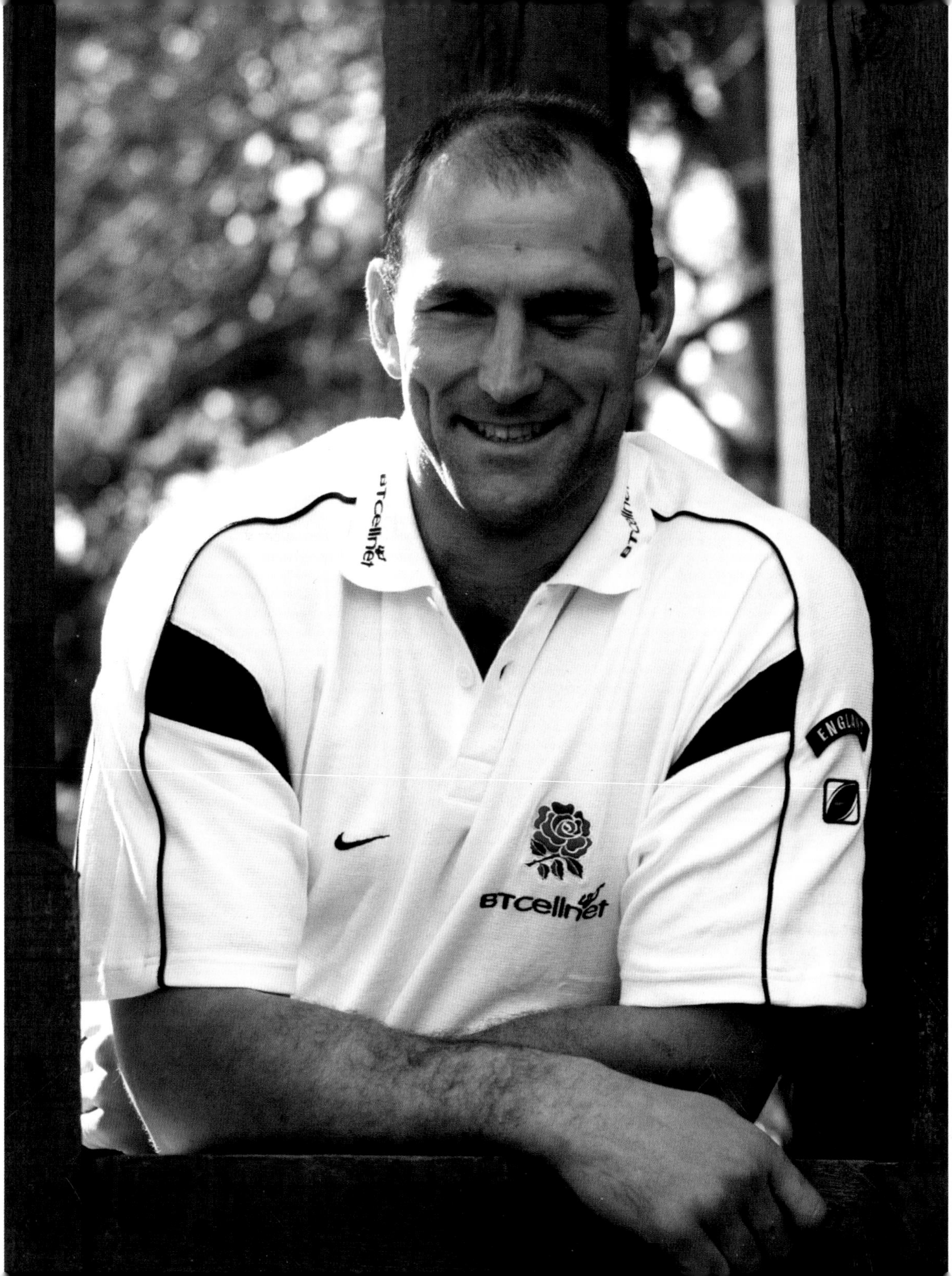
BTcellnet

left A good day at the office. Dallaglio models the latest England shirt.

above 'I was sure I packed my gum shield.'

Land of his father. Dallaglio, flanked by Matt Dawson, Jason Leonard and Martin Johnson, comes on as substitute during England's mauling of Italy in Rome in the 2002 Six Nations.

LAWRENCE DALLAGLIO

Scoring against the Italians in England's 45-9 victory.

above Happy days at Wasps.

right Dallaglio's hopes of a knighthood suddenly looked to be improving. In the dressing room after England's dramatic 31-28 win over New Zealand at Twickenham in November 2002.

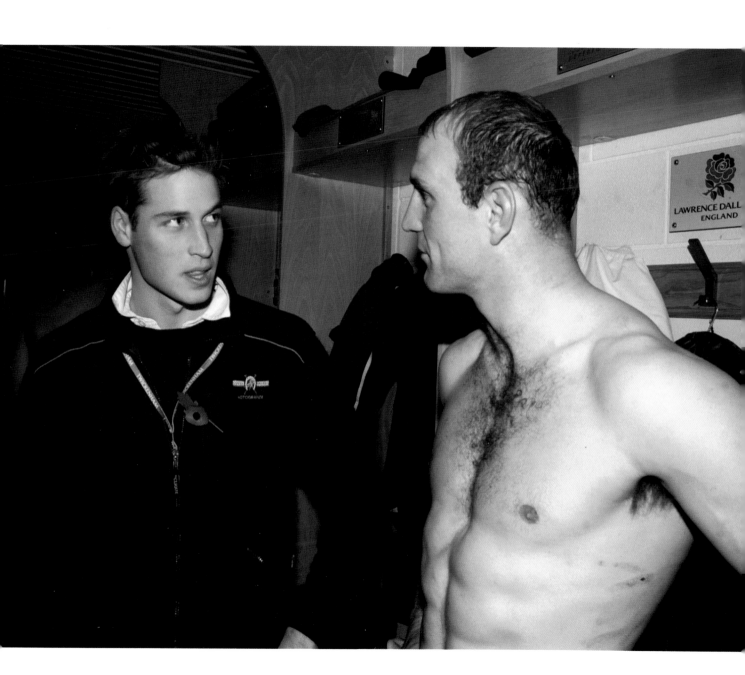

1998-2002

Strength Passion

Intelligence Skill

In honour of a man who has it all. Loans.co.uk would like to thank Lawrence for everything he has done for us, his fans and friends at Loans.co.uk. He has brightened our days and has been a wonderful advertisement for rugby and sport in general. His spirit, charisma and enthusiasm for life is an inspiration to us all. We wish Lawrence a fantastic testimonial year and a long, fulfilling future.

Loans.co.uk

2003

There are times in your sporting life when it doesn't get much better and for Dallaglio this year is worth bottling up and savouring. After all those failures there was a first Grand Slam triumph, plus victories in Wellington against the All Blacks and in Melbourne over the Wallabies. On the club front, victory at Twickenham against Gloucester made Wasps the Zurich Premiership champions which stood alongside their Parker Pen Challenge Cup triumph. And all in World Cup year!

At the heart of those magical moments was Dallaglio. Although he started the Grand Slam season on the bench (yet again) he made a huge impact after replacing Lewis Moody in the 44th minute during the important 25-17 home win over France to get the show on the road. Patently, he was making it clear to coach Woodward that he wasn't going to be content with walk-on parts in this campaign. Woodward took the hint and Dallaglio was once again a huge presence in the England pack as they hurtled towards a Slam decider with Ireland in Dublin. The stage was set for Dallaglio and his team-mates to prove they really were the Northern Hemisphere champions and capable of winning away from Fortress Twickenham - something they would have to do on a regular basis to land the World Cup. 'It's very important that this team go into the World Cup with something tangible to show for our achievements,' said Dallaglio. 'You do not want to be remembered as a very good team who didn't actually win anything.'

The final whistle in Dublin signalled uncontained joy in English ranks as the ghosts of past defeats were exorcised with a 42-6 victory, begun by Dallaglio's try. Not even a remarkable spat before the anthems (when England refused to move to allow the Irish to stand in their place) could detract from the day. 'There was a real determination within the team to win the Slam right up to the final whistle,' said Dallaglio. 'I did say we should be shot if we don't win something in 2003 and so I am thankful we have! We can now move on and you can't underestimate the confidence that winning this match will give us.'

It was enough to silence the Southern Hemisphere moaners for a while until they came up with the same old 'Dad's Army' taunts before the wins over the All Blacks and Wallabies in their own backyards in June. That took England to thirteen successive wins and another followed in the World Cup warm-up with Wales before France won in Marseilles. The return with the French at Twickenham a week later was the moment for Woodward to stop experimenting and bring out the big guns and that meant Dallaglio was back on home turf and raring to go. Of course, this commitment to England's World Cup cause meant Dallaglio had to remove himself from his beloved Wasps team until the tournament was over. Dallaglio has heard it all: the snide comments about Wasps only winning the Zurich title by default; that Gloucester are the real champions in 2003 because they finished fifteen points ahead of Wasps in the table before the play-offs. 'Hogwash' is one reply that can be repeated in a family book! 'Gloucester had been more consistent but, ultimately, on the big occasion, they were unable to deliver,' said the Wasps captain. 'The game is all about delivering on big occasions. Gloucester were beaten by the best team in this country since Christmas. We won seventeen of our last nineteen matches, we thoroughly deserved to be champions.'

LAWRENCE DALLAGLIO

2003

previous pages:
left Bum note. Dallaglio leaves Ireland's Peter Stringer with an unpleasant taste in his mouth during England's 2003 Six Nations Grand Slam-clinching win at Lansdowne Road.

right Easy does it. Dallaglio scores against the Irish as England conquer their nerves to land the Grand Slam.

these pages:
above Back row battlers. Richard Hill (left), Neil Back (centre) and Dallaglio proudly show off the Six Nations trophy after their victory in Dublin.

right England take an early shower as they celebrate their Six Nations Championship triumph.

2003

left Leader of the pack. Dallaglio flies high as Wasps take on Bath.

right Dallaglio enjoys a friendly debate with Bath lock and England team-mate Steve Borthwick.

LAWRENCE DALLAGLIO

left We are the champions! Dallaglio celebrates Wasps'
Parker Pen Challenge Cup Final win over Bath in May 2003.

below Dallaglio and Wasps team-mate Joe Worsley with the
Parker Pen Challenge Cup.

LAWRENCE DALLAGLIO

left 'Come on, I only want a hug!' Dallaglio ignores the pleas of Gloucester's Andy Gomarsall during the Zurich Premiership Final at Twickenham in May 2003. Wasps won comfortably 39-3.

right Captain fantastic. Lifting the Zurich Premiership trophy.

LAWRENCE DALLAGLIO

Dallaglio and the England team hold their stomachs in to model their new World Cup kit.

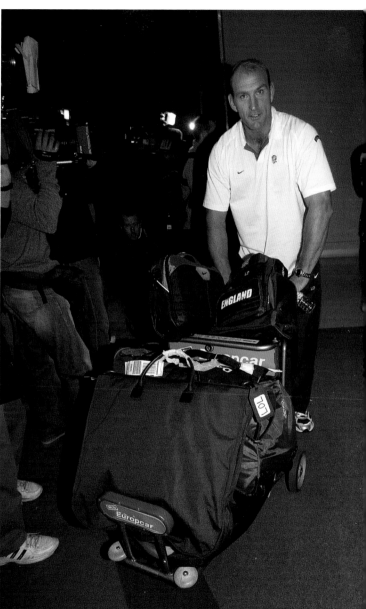

LAWRENCE DALLAGLIO

far left DIY jacuzzi.

left Arriving at Perth Airport for the World Cup.

right Older and wiser. Dallaglio shares his thoughts on England's World Cup campaign.

2003

above Lean on me. Dallaglio and captain Martin Johnson limber up for England's first training session in Australia.

right 'I'd rather face the All Blacks than this lot!' Dallaglio does battle with the press.

far right New balls please. And make them a bit bigger this time.

2003

left Surf's up. Dallaglio, Neil Back (left) and Richard Hill (right) sample the delights of the Australian coastline.

above By George! World Cup minnows Georgia feel the weight of another Dallaglio charge during England's heavy Pool C victory in Perth.

LAWRENCE DALLAGLIO

left Springboks stunned. Dallaglio hunts down Louis Koen as England beat South Africa in their crucial World Cup group clash at the Subiaco Oval in Perth.

right The calm after the storm as Dallaglio and Lewis Moody help each other off the pitch in Perth.

left Dallaglio tells Jonny Wilkinson he wants the kicking duties in the next match.

right Another gruelling England training session!

2003

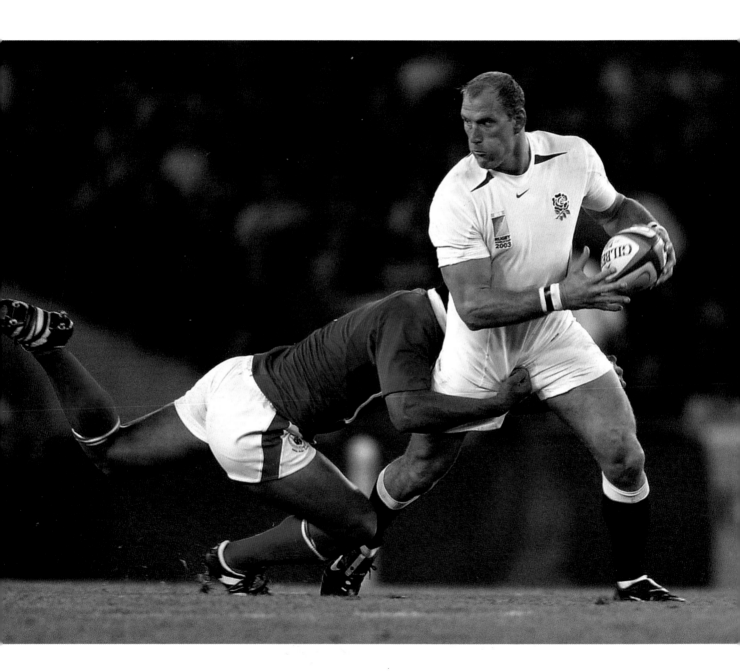

LAWRENCE DALLAGLIO

2003

above and below left In the swing. Dallaglio takes time off as England prepare for their final group game against Uruguay.

right Dallaglio goes down but England still thump Uruguay 111-13 in Brisbane to confirm Clive Woodward's side as group winners.

left Dallaglio and Phil Vickery became closer as the World
Cup progressed.

above 'These Aussie towns are tiny!' Dallaglio sees how he
measures up against the Perth skyline.

These pages
left Dousing the dragon's fire. Dallaglio battles to escape the clutches of Gareth Llewellyn in England's tense quarter-final win over Wales in Brisbane.

right Dallaglio stretches his legs and the Wales defence as England book their place in the semi-finals.

Following pages
left The semi-final. Dallaglio leads the way as England triumph over the French in the battle of the Northern Hemisphere.

right Going nowhere. Dallaglio clings on for dear life as England find their form against Les Bleus to reach the World Cup final.

LAWRENCE DALLAGLIO

2003

left Final flourish. Dallaglio leads the charge as England hold their nerve in a dramatic extra time World Cup final triumph over Australia in Sydney.

right World champion. Dallaglio celebrates England's dramatic extra-time victory in Sydney.

LAWRENCE DALLAGLIO

Iceberg.
Proud to support
Lawrence's
Benefit Year.

Iceberg Marketing plc. Contact: Simon Knibbs 01604 233 222 www.iceberguk.com

Benefit

igroup are proud to support
The Lawrence Dallagio Benefit Year

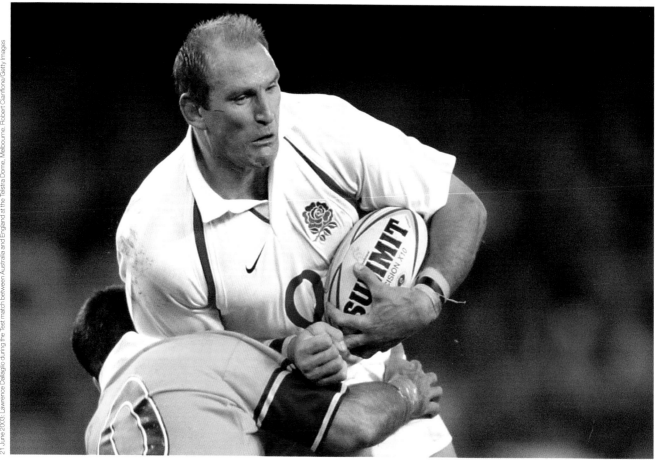

DEFINING THE MOMENT...
ACHIEVEMENT

gettyimages®

We are delighted to offer our congratulations and best wishes to Lawrence in this, his testimonial year

News. Sport. Entertainment. Archive.
gettyimages.com

21 June 2003: Lawrence Dallaglio during the Test match between Australia and England at the Telstra Dome, Melbourne. Robert Cianflone/Getty Images